JOHN RUTTER

THE SPRIG OF THYME

A CYCLE OF FOLK-SONG SETTINGS
FOR MIXED CHOIR WITH CHAMBER ENSEMBLE
(OR CHAMBER ORCHESTRA)

T0056999

MUSIC DEPARTMENT

OXFORD
UNIVERSITY PRESS

UNIVERSITY PRESS

Great Clarendon Street, Oxford OX2 6DP, England
198 Madison Avenue, New York, NY10016, USA

Oxford is a registered trademark of Oxford University Press

© Oxford University Press 1994

All rights reserved. No part of this publication may be
reproduced, stored in a retrieval system, or transmitted,
in any form or by any means, electronic, mechanical,
photocopying, recording, or otherwise, without the prior
permission in writing of Oxford University Press.

Permission to perform this work in public (except in the
course of divine worship) should normally be obtained
from the performing Right Society Ltd. (PRS), 29/33 Berners
Street, London W1T 3AB, or its affiliated Societies in each
country throughout the world, unless the owner or the
occupier of the premises being used holds a licence
from the society.

Permission to make a recording must be obtained in
advance from the Mechanical Copyright Protection Society
Ltd. (MCPS), Elgar House, 41 Streatham High Road, London
SW16 1ER, or its affiliated Societies in each country
throughout the world.

Instrumentation

Flute
Oboe
Clarinet in B flat and A
Bassoon
Harp
Violin 1
Violin 2
Viola
Cello
Bass

The string parts are intended for one player per part, but they
can be doubled if the work is performed by chamber orchestra.

Instrumentation of the individual numbers is as follows:

Page

1	1.	The bold grenadier: fl, ob, cl, bsn, hp, 2 vln, vla, vc, cb
5	2.	The keel row: fl, ob, cl, bsn
12	3.	The willow tree: hp, 2 vln, vla, vc, cb
16	4.	The sprig of thyme: 2 vln, vla, vc
19	5.	Down by the sally gardens: cl, 2 vln, vla, vc, cb
22	6.	The cuckoo: hp
29	7.	I know where I'm going: ob, 2 vln, vla, vc
32	8.	Willow song: unaccompanied
34	9.	O can ye sew cushions?: fl, hp, 2 vln, vla, vc, cb
37	10.	The miller of Dee: ob, cl, bsn
41	11.	Afton water: fl, ob, hp, 2 vln, vla, vc, cb

All performing material is available on hire from the publisher.

All eleven numbers from *The Sprig of Thyme* have been
recorded by the Cambridge Singers and members of the City of
London Sinfonia, directed by John Rutter, on the album *The
Sprig of Thyme* (Collegium Records CD CSCD 517).

Duration: 35 minutes

Conductors may wish to select short groups of songs from *The
Sprig of Thyme* for performance with specific instruments. For
example, *The keel row* plus *The miller of Dee* requires only
woodwind quartet; *The sprig of thyme* plus *I know where I'm
going* requires oboe and string quartet; *The willow tree* plus *The
cuckoo* requires harp and string quintet. *Willow song*, being
unaccompanied, can be added to any selected group. (JR)

The sprig of thyme, I know where I'm going, and *O can ye sew
cushions?* are also published together as *Three folk-songs for
upper voices* (U167).
Down by the sally gardens and *The miller of Dee* are also
published together as *Two folk-songs for male voices* (M23).

THE SPRIG OF THYME

arranged by
JOHN RUTTER

1. The bold grenadier

English folk-song

© Oxford University Press 1994

Printed in Great Britain

OXFORD UNIVERSITY PRESS, MUSIC DEPARTMENT, GREAT CLARENDON STREET, OXFORD OX2 6DP

Photocopying this copyright music is ILLEGAL.

bold gren - a - dier.

TENORS and BASSES *mp* **A** *poco cresc.*

2. 'Good morn-ing, good morn-ing, good

morn-ing,' said he: 'O— where are you go - ing, my pret-ty là - dy?' 'I am go-ing a-

mf **SOPRANOS and ALTOS** *mf*

walk - ing by the clear cry - stal stream, To see cool wa - ters glide and hear night-in - gales

mp *p legato*

sing.

B (S. and A.) *mf più animato*

3. O sol-dier, O— sol-dier, will you mar - ry

cresc. *mf* *poco agitato*

3

4

2. The keel row

Northumbrian folk-song

3. The willow tree

Andante (♩ = *c*. 76)

English folk-song

1. O take me to your arms, love, for keen doth the wind blow, O take me to your arms, love, for bitter is my deep woe. She hears me not, she heeds me not, nor will she listen to me, While here I lie alone to

TENORS *mp*

Hum

TENORS and BASSES unis. *mp*

(Hum)

die be - neath the wil - low tree.

2. My love hath wealth and beau - ty, rich_ suit - ors at - tend her door, My___ love hath wealth and

beau-ty, she slights me be-cause I'm_ poor. The_ rib-bon fair that bound her hair is_

all_ that is left_ to_ me, While_ here I lie a - lone_ to die be - neath the wil-low tree.

Hum

3. I once had gold and sil - ver, I_ thought them with -

(Hum)

TENORS
only *mp*

-out— end, I— once had gold and sil - ver, I thought— I had a true friend. My

D (TENORS)

wealth is lost, my friend is false, my love— hath he sto - len from— me, While—

sim.

rall. al fine

p   dim.   *pp*

here I lie a - lone— to die be - neath the wil - low tree.

pp

Ped.   *

4. The sprig of thyme

(*sopranos only*)

Lincolnshire folk-song

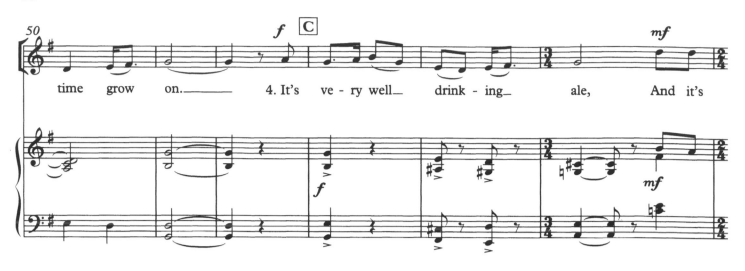

time grow on._____ 4. It's ve - ry well___ drink - ing___ ale, And it's

Poco meno mosso

ve - ry well drink - ing wine:_____ But it's far bet - ter sit - ting by a

rit.

young man's side That_____ has won this___ heart of___ mine.

5. Down by the sally gardens

(tenors and basses)

Words by W. B. YEATS

Irish traditional melody

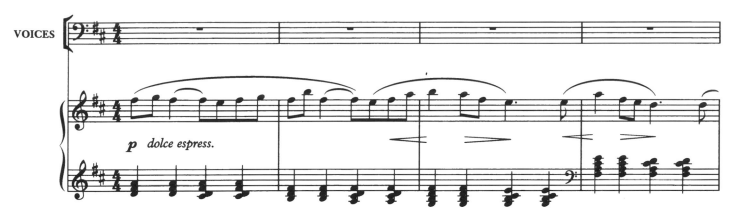

bid me take love ea - sy, As the leaves grow on the tree. But I be-ing young and

fool - ish, With her did not a - gree.

2. In a field by the ri - - ver My love and I did

stand. And on my lean - ing shoul - der She placed her snow - white

6. The cuckoo

English folk-song

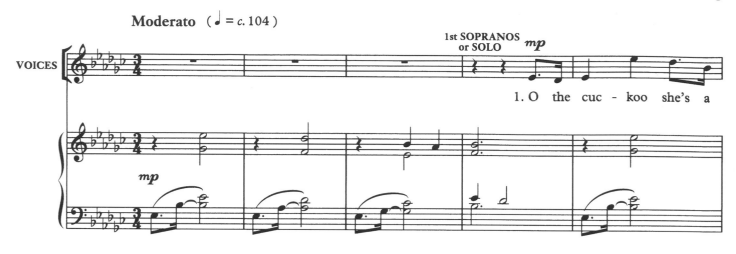

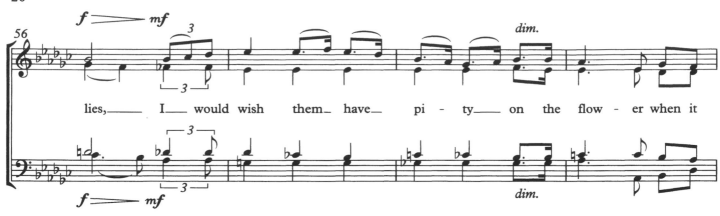

lies,___ I___ would wish them__ have__ pi – ty___ on the flow - er when it

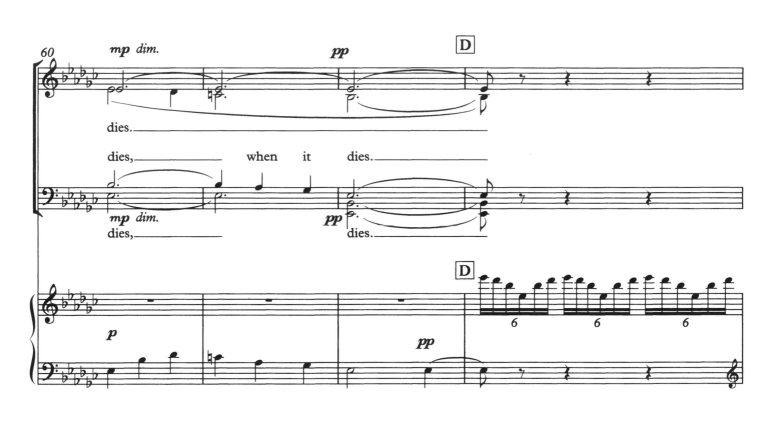

dies.___

dies,___ when it dies.___

dies,___ dies.___

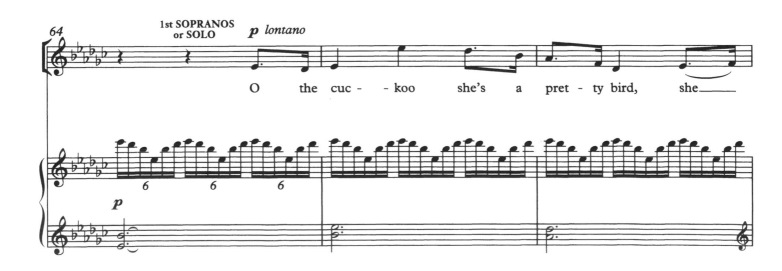

1st SOPRANOS
or SOLO

O the cuc – -koo she's a pret - ty bird, she___

7. I know where I'm going

(sopranos only)

Irish folk-song

soft, And paint-ed rooms are bon-ny, But I would leave them all__ To__ go with my love

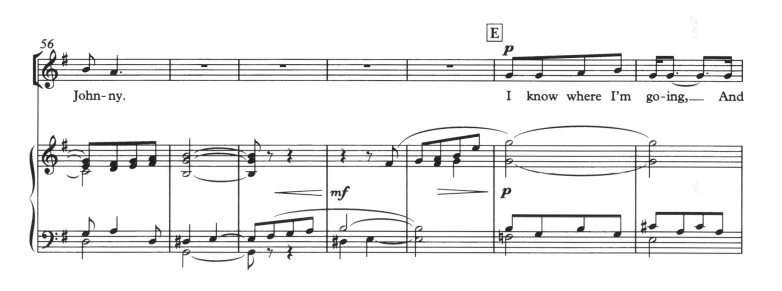

John-ny.

I know where I'm go-ing,__ And

Meno mosso

I know who's going with me, I know who I love__ But the dear knows who I'll mar-ry.

8. Willow song

(A poor soul sat sighing)

16th-century melody and words

9. O can ye sew cushions?

(sopranos and altos)

Scottish folk-song

Gently (♩ = *c.* 92)

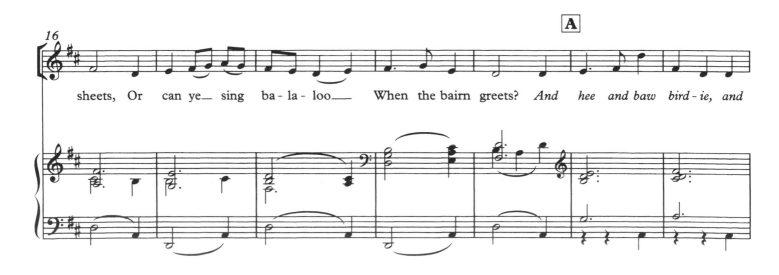

hee and baw lamb, And hee and baw bird - ie, my bon - ny wee lamb.

2. I placed my cra - dle On yon hol - ly top, And ay as the

wind blew My cra - dle did rock. And hush - a - baw bird - ie, and ba - li - lee

loo, And hee and baw bird - ie, my bon - ny wee doo.

And hee and baw bird - ie, and hee and baw lamb, And hee and baw

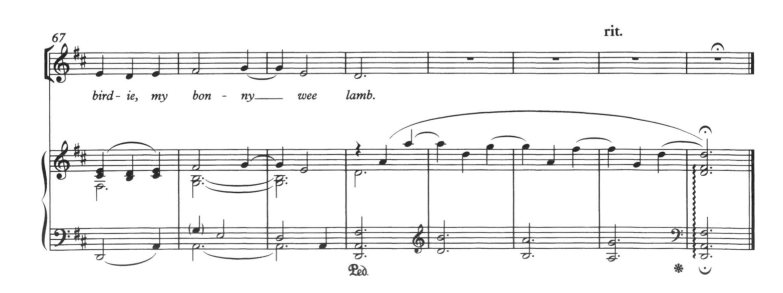

bird - ie, my bon - ny —— wee lamb.

10. The miller of Dee

(tenors and basses)

English traditional song

1. There was a jol-ly mill-er once, Lived on the Riv-er Dee.___ He danced and sang from morn till night, No lark more blithe than he.___ And this the bur-den of his song For-ev-er used to be:___ 'I

care for no-bo-dy, no, not I, If no-bo-dy cares for me.

love my mill, she is to me Both pa-rent, child and wife.

I would not change my sta-tion for An-o-ther one in life. Then

11. Afton water

Scottish folk-song

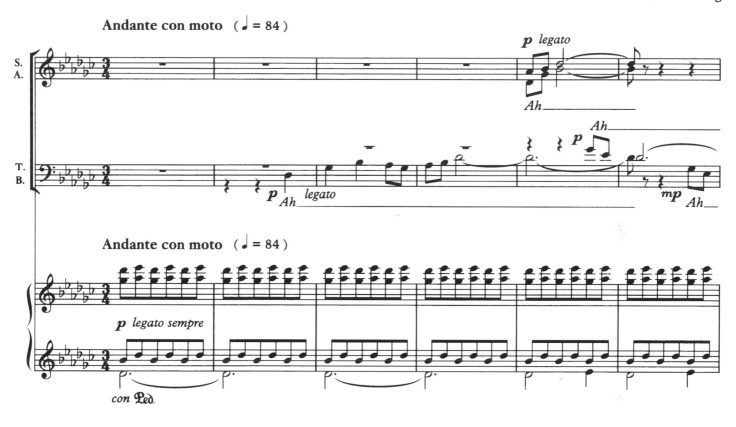

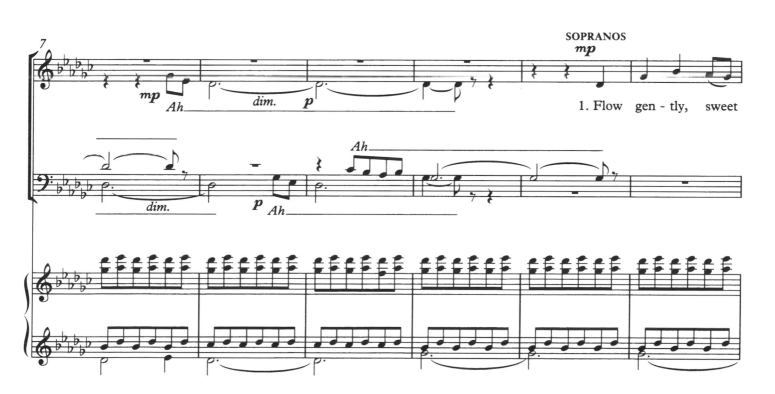

13

Af - ton, a - mong thy green braes,— Flow gen - tly, I'll— sing thee a— song in— thy—

19

TENORS

SOPRANOS and TENORS

mp

p

praise. My— Ma - ry's a - sleep by thy mur-mur-ing stream, Flow gen - tly, sweet

25

A

Af - ton, dis - turb not— her— dream.

mp
dolce

2. How loft-y, sweet Af-ton, thy_ neigh-bour-ing_ hills,_ Far marked with the_

TENORS and BASSES *unis.*

Aw _____ *Aw* __

There dai-ly_ I_ wan-der as dawn ri - ses_

cours-es of_ clear wind-ing_ rills.

high,_ My flocks and my_ Ma - ry's sweet cot in_ my_ eye._

3. How— plea-sant thy— banks and— green val-leys be - low,— Where

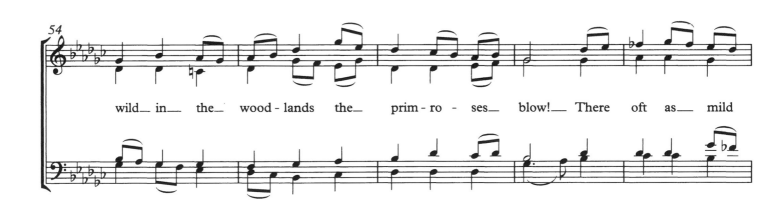

wild— in the— wood-lands the— prim-ro-ses— blow!— There oft as— mild

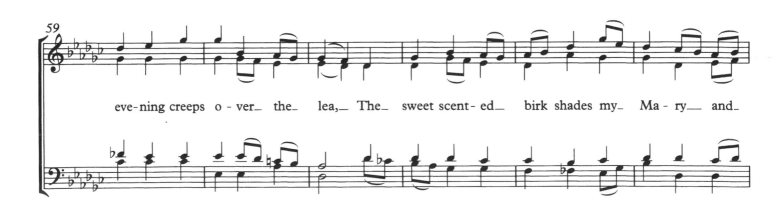

eve-ning creeps o - ver— the— lea,— The— sweet scent-ed— birk shades my— Ma - ry— and—

46

-sleep by thy mur-mur-ing_ stream, Flow gen-tly, sweet Af-ton, dis-turb not_ her_

dream.

Printed in England by Caligraving Limited Thetford Norfolk